BIBLE EXPLORERS

The Life of Jesus

Leena Lane - Gillian Chapman

Jesus is born

An angel brought good news to Mary: 'You will have a baby! Call him Jesus. He will be God's son!'

Mary and her husband Joseph had to travel a very long way to Bethlehem. There was nowhere for them to stay: all the inns in the town were full. So they settled down with the animals in a warm room behind the inn. Jesus – God's own son – was born. Mary wrapped him up warmly and placed him in a manger.

That night, shepherds on the hills near Bethlehem had a great surprise. An angel appeared, saying, 'Don't be afraid! I bring good news for you and all the world. Today in Bethlehem your Saviour is born. Go and find him. He is wrapped in cloths and lying in a manger.'

The shepherds hurried to find the baby. They praised God for what they had seen.

Wise men came from the east, looking for a new king. They brought gifts of gold, frankincense and myrrh to Jesus and worshipped him.

Luke 2, verses 4 to 20;
Matthew 2, verses 1 to 12

Something to think about:

All new babies are special, but what was so special about Jesus?

Activity:

These animals were born in a stable too. Can you complete the pictures?

Activity:

Can you find four mistakes in this picture of Mary and Joseph?

Prayer:

Dear God, thank you for sending Jesus to be born as a baby. Help me to remember him all year round, not just at Christmas.

Where is Jesus?

When Jesus was twelve years old, he went to Jerusalem with Mary and Joseph for the Passover feast. Many people from his home town went together. It was a great celebration.

When it was time to go home, Jesus stayed behind in Jerusalem. But Mary and Joseph did not notice. They thought he was playing with his friends. Mary began to get very worried and they turned back to Jerusalem to look for Jesus.

Three days later, they found Jesus. He was in the temple courts, speaking to a group of teachers. Everyone was amazed at the things Jesus said. He seemed to know so much about God.

'My son!' said Mary. 'Don't you know how worried we have been?'

'Mother,' said Jesus, 'didn't you know I would be here in my Father's house?'

But Mary and Joseph did not understand what he meant.

Luke 2, verses 41 to 52

Activity:

Cross out the birds which were not sacrificed in the temple:

flamingos pigeons robins

Something to think about:

Why did Jesus call the temple 'my Father's house'?

Prayer:

Dear God, help me to learn more about you.

Activity:

Can you colour in this picture of Mary and Joseph?

Activity:

Can you find the matching pair of candle stands?

Jesus is baptised

John the Baptist told people to be prepared for the coming of God's kingdom.

'Say sorry to God for all the wrong things you have done, and be baptised!' he said.

✎ Activity:

Colour in the dotted pieces of this picture and see what you can find.

John baptised them in the River Jordan as a sign of God washing their sins away.

When Jesus was about thirty years old, he came to see John on the bank of the river.

'I want you to baptise me in the river,' said Jesus.

John was very surprised. He knew that Jesus had done nothing wrong so he didn't need to be baptised. But Jesus asked him again and John baptised him.

When Jesus came out of the river, heaven opened and he saw a dove, and a voice spoke: 'This is my dear son, with whom I am pleased.'

It was God's voice speaking.

Matthew 3, verses 13 to 17

Prayer:

Dear God, I am sorry for the wrong things I have done, especially... Thank you that you forgive me when I am sorry.

Something to think about:

God loves to forgive us when we say sorry.

Activity:

Match the picture details and write their identification letters in the correct boxes.

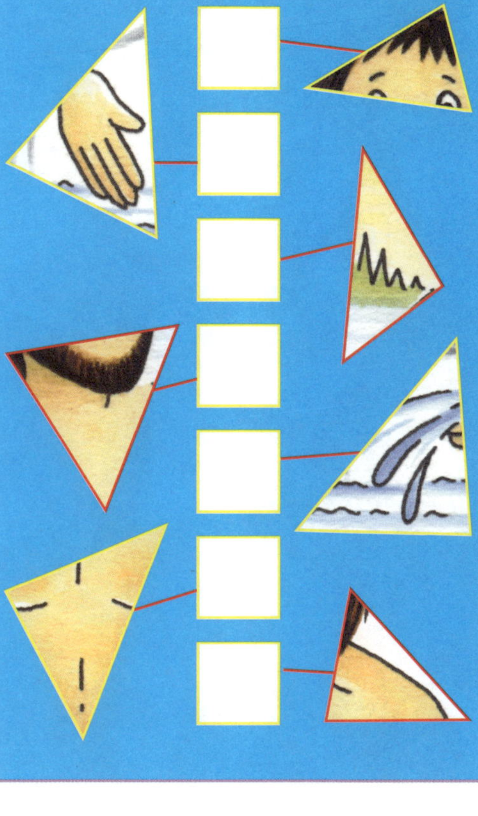

Jesus is tested

Something to think about:

Jesus used words from the Bible when he was tested. Do you know any words from the Bible by heart?

After Jesus was baptised, he was led by God into the desert and ate nothing for forty days and nights. The devil came and tested Jesus.

First the devil told Jesus to turn stones into bread.

But Jesus replied with words from Scripture, saying, 'People cannot live on bread alone, but need every word that God has spoken.'

Then the devil took Jesus to the top of the temple and told him to throw himself off so that the angels would catch him.

But Jesus replied: 'It is written, "Do not put God to the test."'

Lastly the devil took Jesus to a high mountain and promised to give Jesus all the kingdoms of the earth, if he would only bow down and worship him. But Jesus did not give in.

'It is written, "Worship the Lord your God and serve him alone,"' he said. Then the devil went away. Angels came to be with Jesus.

Matthew 4, verses 1 to 11

Activity:

Which words in the list below describe Jesus? Underline them in red. Which words describe the devil? Underline them in black.

wicked	liar
proud	humble
truthful	good
cunning	hungry
loving	selfish

Prayer:

Dear God, please help me to talk to you when I am being tested or in a difficult situation.

Jesus the King

Jesus and his friends were on their way to Jerusalem for the Passover festival.

Jesus sent two of his friends on ahead, saying, 'Go to the village over there and find a young donkey. Bring it to me. Say that your master needs it.'

The two friends fetched the donkey, put their cloaks over the donkey's back and Jesus sat on it.

Jesus rode into the great city of Jerusalem. Huge

Something to think about:
Jesus was a king, but he rode into Jerusalem on a donkey. Why?

Activity:

Can you find the ten differences in the picture opposite?

crowds came to greet him, spreading their cloaks on the road and waving palm branches. They greeted him as their King.

'Hosanna!' they shouted. 'Blessed is he who comes in the name of the Lord!'

Some teachers from the temple were angry with Jesus. They wanted to get rid of him. But Jesus entered Jerusalem and went to the temple.

Mark 11, verses 1 to 11

Prayer:

Dear God, thank you for sending Jesus to be the King of Kings.

The last supper

Jesus met his twelve friends at the upper room of a house in Jerusalem. He washed his disciples' feet, then reclined at the table with his friends, ready to eat the Passover meal.

Jesus looked at his friends gathered round him and said, 'One of you is going to hand me over to be killed.'

It would be Judas Iscariot.

Jesus took some bread, broke it and gave it to his friends. 'Eat this and remember me,' said Jesus. 'This is my body.'

Then he took the cup of wine, thanked God for it, and handed it round. 'Drink this and remember me,' said Jesus. 'This is my blood, given for many.'

They sang a song to God, then went to the Mount of Olives to pray.

Mark 14, verses 12 to 26

Prayer:

Dear God, help me to remember all that Jesus did for us.

Something to think about:

How do Christians still remember Jesus giving the bread and wine?

✎ Activity:

Can you draw some cups and plates on the table?

✎ Activity:

Locate each person at the table. Connect them with a line. Which one is not at the table?

Jesus in the garden

On the Mount of Olives was a garden called Gethsemane. Here Jesus knelt down to pray to God. He knew that the time was coming for him to be taken away from his friends. Tears ran down his face as he prayed to God, his Father in heaven.

Jesus asked his friends to pray with him. But they kept falling asleep.

'Why are you sleeping?' he asked them. 'Watch and pray with me.'

Suddenly a crowd came towards them, and Judas Iscariot was with them. Soldiers and chief priests followed closely behind. Judas came near to Jesus to kiss him. This showed the soldiers where Jesus was.

Jesus was arrested and taken away to see the High Priest.

Mark 14, verses 32 to 50

Activity:

Can you find the one matching pair of butterflies? Put a circle around them.

Prayer:

Dear God, please help me to watch and pray for the people around me and the things I see.

Something to think about:

If you had been with Jesus, would you have prayed with him or fallen asleep?

Activity:

Make a pattern on the butterfly wings and colour it in to make a beautiful butterfly for the garden.

Jesus on trial

Jesus was brought before Pilate, the Roman governor.

'What has this man done wrong?' Pilate asked the crowd.

'He is causing trouble all over the country,' said the chief priests. 'He says he is a king.'

'Are you the King of the Jews?' asked Pilate.

'Yes, it is as you say,' said Jesus.

'What shall I do with Jesus?' Pilate asked the crowd.

'Put him on a cross to die!' the people shouted.

Pilate did not think Jesus had done anything wrong, but he wanted to please the crowd. So he handed Jesus over to

Activity: What is this man's name?

___ ___ ___ ___ t ___

the soldiers to be killed. His soldiers put a purple robe on Jesus and a crown of thorns on his head.

Mark 15, verses 1 to 17

Something to think about:

Pilate tried to please the crowd, rather than doing what he thought was the fair thing to do. Do you ever listen to what people think rather than doing what's right?

Prayer:

Dear God, I am sorry for times when I have not been fair to other people.

Activity:

Can you answer all these questions about Jesus?

How many presents did the wise men bring for baby Jesus? (See page 2)	
On what page can you find a small picture of an angel?	
How old was Jesus when his parents lost him in the temple? (See page 4)	
How many people ate at the Passover meal? (See page 13 and count them)	
How many friends was Jesus was betrayed by? (See page 14)	
How many things did the soldiers give Jesus to wear? (The answer is on this page)	
Add up all the answers above to find out how old Jesus was when he died.	

Jesus dies on a cross

Jesus was taken by the soldiers to a place called Golgotha. There he was nailed to a cross. Above his head was a sign which said 'The King of the Jews'.

Jesus' mother, Mary, stood close by and watched. Darkness covered the land. At the ninth hour, Jesus cried out in a loud voice to God, then breathed his last breath. Jesus died.

Jesus' body was taken down from the cross. It was wrapped in cloths and carefully placed in a tomb belonging to Joseph of Arimathea. A very heavy round stone was rolled across the doorway of the tomb.

Jesus' friends thought they would never see him again. They went home and wept.

Mark 15, verses 20 to 47

Prayer:

Dear God, help me to understand more about what Jesus did for us.

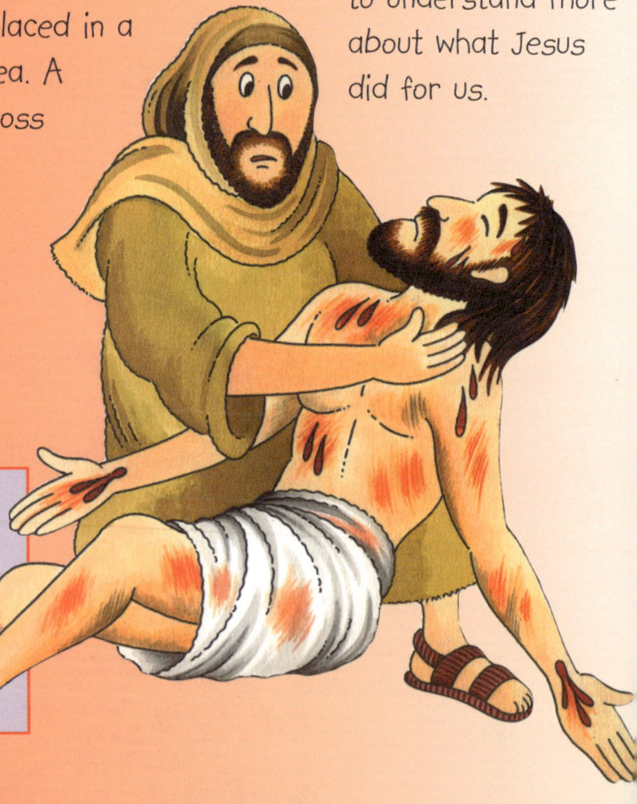

Something to think about:

Have you ever wondered why Jesus had to die on a cross?

Activity:

Can you find these words?

- JESUS
- GOLGOTHA
- MARY
- JOSEPH
- TOMB
- DARK

Q	M	I	N	S	F	P	D
J	G	I	Y	J	S	P	A
O	O	G	U	E	S	Y	R
S	L	C	R	A	L	S	K
E	G	J	E	S	U	S	A
P	O	O	T	O	M	B	C
H	T	S	D	U	A	F	E
T	H	E	R	S	R	I	S
H	A	P	E	Z	Y	S	U
O	T	H	S	I	A	H	R

Activity:

Darkness covered the land before Jesus died.

Can you tell what these silhouettes are?

Jesus is alive!

Three sad days passed.

Early on Sunday morning, some of the women went to his tomb with special spices. What a shock they had when they got there! The large stone which blocked the entrance to the tomb had been rolled away! The tomb was empty!

Jesus' body had gone. All that was left were the strips of cloth which Jesus' body had been wrapped in.

Suddenly two men in bright shining clothes appeared.

'Don't look for Jesus here,' they said. 'He is alive!'

The women ran home at once and told Jesus' friends.

Over the next few days, Jesus appeared to all his disciples. At first, some were not sure it was Jesus. Some did not believe until they saw the wounds in Jesus' hands. But soon everyone knew – Jesus really was alive!

Luke 24, verses 1 to 43

Activity:

Can you help Mary find the right way to the tomb?

Prayer:

Dear God, thank you for making Jesus come alive again so that we can know him too!

Something to think about:

Would you have believed that Jesus was alive again?

Jesus returns to heaven

Jesus saw his friends many times over the next few days.

'Don't leave Jerusalem,' he told his disciples, 'but wait for the gift which God has promised to give you – the Holy Spirit. When he comes, you will be able to tell the whole world about me!'

After forty days, Jesus was taken up to heaven. He was hidden from sight by a cloud.

As the disciples were looking at the sky, two men in white clothes stood beside them.

'Why are you looking at the sky?' they asked the disciples. 'Jesus will return one day in the same way as you saw him go.'

Acts 1, verses 1 to 11

Activity:

On what page can you find a blue dragonfly? ☐

Something to think about:

Who do you think the men in white clothes were?

Activity:

Find and mark the odd one out.

Activity:

Find and circle three of a kind.

Prayer:

Dear God, thank you that Jesus will come back again one day. Help me to be ready for him.

Published in the UK by
The Bible Reading Fellowship
First Floor, Elsfield Hall, 15-17 Elsfield Way, Oxford OX2 8FG
ISBN 1 84101 453 2

First edition 2005

Editorial Director Annette Reynolds
Art Director Gerald Rogers
Pre-production Krystyna Hewitt
Production John Laister

British Library Cataloguing in Publication Data.
A catalogue record for this book is available from the British Library.

Printed and bound in Singapore